Media Guide *for* Academics

by
Joann Ellison Rodgers &
William C. Adams

Production of the *Media Guide for Academics* was funded
in part by the **W.K. Kellogg Foundation**

Published by the Foundation for American Communications (FACS)
3800 Barham Boulevard, Suite 409 • Los Angeles, CA • 90068

Copyright © 1994 by the Foundation For American Communications (FACS).
All rights reserved.

Library of Congress Catalog Card Number: 94-61228

THE FOUNDATION FOR AMERICAN COMMUNICATIONS (FACS) is an independent, non-profit educational institution providing knowledge, resources and perspectives needed by journalists and their sources to effectively communicate, through the news, information about important public issues. Since 1979, thousands of journalists have attended FACS mid-career educational conferences sponsored by news organizations and philanthropic foundations. FACS also provides education in the news process for leaders in business, nonprofit organizations and universities, and organizes Forums for journalists and newsmakers to discuss major issues in the news.

Contents

Preface 1

Introduction
Going Public
    Who? Me? 5

Chapter 1
Why Spread the Word?
    Nine Good Reasons to Talk to a Journalist 9

Chapter 2
Why Journalists Act the Way They Do
    Three Common Hypotheses and Four Standards 17

Chapter 3
Support Your PIO
    Nine Ways to Work Together 27

Chapter 4
Specifics in Working With the Media
    At Least Three Dozen Ways 35

Chapter 5
Strategic Communications
    Eleven Tactics for Big Issues 47

Chapter 6
Crisis Communications
    Thirteen Ways of Making Lemonade 53

Chapter 7
Nine Questions Academics Frequently Ask
    Twelve Reasonable Answers 61

Bibliography 69

PREFACE
Academics and Journalists: Ground Zero?

I began my journalism career at the Navy's *All Hands* magazine at the height of the cold war. I sat at a desk near a wall of windows that looked out and down on the Pentagon, about a thousand yards away. The Soviets weren't known for accuracy in those days; they were reputed to have aimed somewhere between one and two hundred missiles at that building.

> *Whereas you can only be nuked once, generally speaking, you can be blown all out of proportion time and time again.*

But not to worry! There were signs posted in all the hallways, telling us exactly what to do in case of a nuclear attack. We were supposed to crawl under our desks. Canned water and biscuits were stored in the basement; as soon as we could we were to make our way down to Quantico, Virginia, where we would receive new assignments.

Now, I concede that there are certain differences between a missile attack and a visit by a reporter or a television crew. Whereas you can only be nuked once, generally speaking, you can be blown all out of proportion time and time again. Still, the media's aim is probably not all that much different from that of the guys who used to live in silos in Siberia; and the media, like the Russians, have the advantage of numbers. There are a LOT of reporters out there, looking for some place to explode, and your chances of getting the attention of one increases with every fresh new journalist who goes through my reporting class. Finally, before the metaphor totally breaks down, there is the issue of terror. To judge from the war stories my academic friends tell about their contacts with the press, the media and the missiles have one last thing in common. Both have an uncanny ability to focus the mind.

> *To many reporters "tomorrow" is a strategic concept.*

Missile attacks, of course, have few silver linings while journalists, despite the protests of the post-modernists, are an essentially neutral force. Though the "attack reporter" does exist and the profession does attract people with a low threshold for blood lust, and while horror stories play an important role in the education of both reporter and source, the average news hound is simply out to get the story. That story is usually innocuously informative, and it generally comes off with minimal trauma to both sides. If in the process there is good or harm done to you or your institution, it's simple happenstance.

If managing that risk factor is notoriously difficult for people in the academic community, it's because the academic frame of reference is so different from the reporter's. The two worlds are almost a perfect mismatch. The best academics think not in years but in decades or centuries, while to many reporters "tomorrow" is a strategic concept. The best intellectuals painstakingly match theory and data, while reporters think in gestalt and write in quick, broad strokes.

Academics, though not without feelings, live the life of the mind; reporters, though generally quite intelligent, are almost without exception adrenaline junkies. Thanks to this clash of cultures, the reporter often seems to the academic to proceed without rhyme or reason; in this, appearances are deceiving. In fact, the most distinctive thing about the journalism life is that everything has a reason. The pressures are so high, and often so immediate, that the real professional rarely makes a superfluous motion. There are roses in a reporter's life, but they too frequently go unsniffed.

Here, then, is the key to understanding journalists. They follow rules, or if not rules, then traditions, patterns, mnemonic checklists: Who, what, when, where, why.

The academic who devotes serious thought to these matters will gain a distinct advantage. You have more time to think about them than they have to think about you, and once you get beyond the alien nature of the media world it turns out to be quite predictable.

After all, a good reporter does what he or she does precisely because he or she understands the system and knows how it will react. When a reporter files a story he or she has a pretty good idea what the city desk will do with it and where it will be played. A good reporter knows how editors will act because he or she has studied them. If you study him, you will be likewise enlightened; and such study is, after all, what the academic is supposed to be about. Academics who put a minimal amount of effort into the problem of the media are not likely to become its casualties.

The value of a book like this is as an introduction and a tour guide of the world of the journalist. It comes to you from the Foundation for American Communications (FACS), a group of people with vast experience educating journalists in matters of substance and helping news sources learn how to communicate their stories. The bits and pieces of information it contains are interesting and worthwhile, but what is priceless is the gestalt. It will give you a peek into a world that is both alien and important, and that you may find surprisingly interesting. But for better or worse, the information age is focusing new attention on the role of the academic in American life. Given our culture's historical ambivalence toward intellectual values, the moment is rife with both possibilities and dangers. Most academics sense that dichotomy at one level or another, and it's probably what led you to pick up this book.

The media are at your door, or, if they aren't, they may be there tomorrow. Like those of us who once wrote Navy propaganda from ground zero, whether we approve isn't very relevant. We can't ignore the information age, and it obviously won't help to crawl under the desk.

> Jon Franklin
> Professor of Journalism
> University of Oregon
> Philomath, Oregon

Following that introduction to journalism in the Navy, Jon Franklin went on to a distinguished newspaper career. As a reporter for The Evening Sun in Baltimore, he won two Pulitzer prizes—the first in 1979 for feature writing and the second in 1985 for explanatory journalism. He currently teaches, lectures and is the author of five books.

INTRODUCTION
Going Public: Who? Me?

> *Journalists create reality...By our reports collectively we construct a picture of the world that becomes the cornerstone of public perceptions from which actions and judgments follow. By so doing, journalists are the architects of the future.*
>
> — Joan Konner, Dean
> Columbia University Graduate
> School of Journalism

On June 24, 1993, before a learned society in Cambridge, England, Princeton University mathematician Andrew Wiles announced he had solved one of the most persistent mysteries of science: Fermat's Last Theorem.

Pierre de Fermat, a 17th century genius, had proposed the equation that X to the power of n, plus Y to the power of n, never equals Z to the power of n if n is a whole number greater than 2. Adding suspense and romance to the theorem's deceptive simplicity, Fermat had scribbled what would become a 300-year-long dare in the margin of a book. He noted that he had worked out the mathematical proof of the equation, but had no room at that moment to write it down.

Cracking the riddle of the theorem carried all the elements of a good news story. Here was history, scientific drama, heroic persistence, the very essence of academic excellence. Professor Wiles could stand as a model for young Newtons.

So what happened when a Reuters news service reporter sought out the professor to tell his story? How did he answer questions about how he did it, how long it took, what drove him? Wiles sent back a message saying that he was "not available for comment."

Unfortunately, when it comes to communicating news of academic achievement, such stories are not uncommon. Some years ago, Phil Boffey of *The New York Times* summed up the frustration of journalists when he told a group of academics at Johns Hopkins University: "You are the first to complain when I write something you don't like or something that's wrong. But you are the last to return my call when I need you to teach, explain and communicate."

Phil Boffey knows that academics are part of a culture that has long been indifferent to what the public understands about their work. In fact, surveys indicate that "going public" ranks low on the academic reward scale.

The Changing View

Fortunately that view is beginning to change and academics are opening up. They see that communicating is a smart thing to do—it pays off in improved public understanding and helps promote academic funding and research.

The evidence of this changing attitude shows up in the increasing quantity of scientific reporting, in the explosive growth of academics writing in the popular press and in the rise in the number of conferences, lectures and workshops on the mass media initiated by scientific societies and other learned groups.

When the Scientific Research Society Sigma Xi held a forum on ethics and values in science, for example, it included these two observations in its conclusions:

- "Scientists and journalists have a mutual responsibility for accurate, open and balanced information."
- "Science must fully disclose to the public its capabilities, limitations and participating role in solving today's social and ethical issues."

This guidebook is designed to help you join that process. It offers some insights into the way journalists work and explains a bit about what mass media and journalism are and are not.

A kind of communication takes place even when the source refuses comment or the journalist doesn't call. (Andrew Wiles, the "no comment" mathematician, let us know precisely what he thought.) But we believe that the best communications are purposeful, strategic and tailored to the needs of the receiver. They are understood by intended audiences. They have an effect. We also believe that communicating through mass media is a learned skill, not a talent. The results of learning that skill do not impede academic effectiveness but enhance it, to the benefit of society.

We believe that it is possible to have impact with integrity.

— William C. Adams &
Joann Ellison Rodgers

CHAPTER ONE

Why Spread the Word?
Nine Good Reasons to Talk to Journalists

When a reporter approaches, I generally find myself wishing for a martini.

— Jonas Salk

Academics accustomed to the careful pace and peer-reviewed precision of scholarship often justifiably complain that much news reporting is neither careful nor precise. They would like popular journalism to reach academic standards, with all the right qualifications and caveats.

These scholars have a ready list of reasons to avoid the press:

- The work is too technical for laymen to understand.
- I don't have the time it would take to explain it.
- The only appropriate place to discuss my work is in peer reviewed journals or in academic meetings. Good scholars don't publish in the press.
- I could lose my grant because my colleagues would think I'm out of line.

- The work is too preliminary.
- My work is pure and basic with no application to any practical endeavor.
- My work is being printed and if I discuss it, the journal won't publish.
- Journalists won't let me see what they write before they print it. As long as they won't be reasonable, why should I spend time on this?
- I've been burned or I know people who have been burned by misleading quotes or misinterpreted explanations.

Journalists counter that they need to produce what one writer called "history on the run." Journalists value speed, timeliness, accuracy, responsiveness and information keyed to the concerns of their audiences.

Clearly these are sharply conflicting cultures. Bringing them together to produce a better informed citizenry can be a true challenge.

What does it take? Certainly tolerance, understanding and generosity of goodwill. It also takes a willingness to learn a few skills.

Philosopher Judith Lichtenberg of the University of Maryland observes that scientists decry the public's lack of understanding, but do much to perpetuate it. She points out that people who can understand mortgage interest rates and baseball statistics can surely find the intellectual energy to understand such equally arcane subjects as philosophy.

Is anyone really hurt if you choose not to try?

Yes. You, your institution, the news media and eventually the public. Here are nine reasons why.

1. You Can Help

Academics now have a relatively small voice in the mass media.
One example: A study conducted by American Opinion Research, Inc. (AOR) for the Foundation for American Communications found that environmental reporters seek information from government sources more than six times as often as they do from academics.

Another study by AOR found that most Americans:

- Get most environmental information from the news media.
- Believe environmental news reporting is done poorly.

In short, the public needs academics to contribute to their understanding of environmental issues. The same can be said of issues of all kinds.

2. At Stake: Scientific Literacy

A study by the American Association for the Advancement of Science suggests that even well educated people are intimidated by the mystique of the academic research process. The study also says there are barriers to public understanding of science, including academic elitism, isolation and arrogance.

Scientific literacy depends on science education, but only a small percentage of high school graduates receive more than a year of science and math, and even fewer have had chemistry, physics or calculus.

Dr. Bruce Alberts, president of the National Academy of Sciences and National Research Council laments, "When you see your children...and you finally pay attention to what they're learning in science...it makes you realize that something's really wrong."

The vast majority of science and humanities education takes place informally, through mass media, and you can begin to have an impact there. You can inspire the next generation of young scientists. You can improve the public's scientific literacy. You can speed progress toward discovery.

3. The Audience Is Ready

Studies indicate that about 20 percent of the adult public is already aware, informed and actively pursuing scientific information about social, physical and biological sciences.

Jon D. Miller, Director of the International Center for the Advancement of Scientific Literacy at the Chicago Academy of Science, calls these people "science attentive." They watch *NOVA* and gobble up such things as *Science Times* in *The New York Times*. Another 20 percent of adults are interested in science; they don't seek out science news but pay attention when it comes.

A 1993 Lou Harris study commissioned by The Scientists' Institute for Public Information found 38 percent read science news at least once a week in newspapers; 40 percent have a weekly conversation with someone else about issues related to science; 43 percent read a book or magazine on science every month and 57 percent watch a TV program on science at least once a week. Interest cuts across all demographic groups.

More than 40 daily newspapers publish weekly science sections. The National Association of Science Writers has more than 2,500 members actively writing for mass audiences. Science journalism programs and fellowships have reached almost 20, including programs based at Harvard, Stanford, Johns Hopkins, MIT and some campuses of the University of California.

4. The Audience Includes Academics

Though some may deny it, academics use the mass media to find out what's going on, even in their own fields. Using the popular press is a way to reach your colleagues.

Sociologist David Phillips of the University of California at San Diego concluded that biomedical researchers get a lot of their information on medical advances from reading the newspaper. He studied scientific citations for articles appearing in *The New England Journal of Medicine* in 1979, and found that a *Journal* study that was picked up and reported on by *The New York Times* got 73 percent more scientific citations in the 10 years after publication than articles that appeared only in the *Journal*.

5. The Audience Can Help Research

One example: A scientist at The Johns Hopkins Oncology Center published an article in *Science* about identification of the gene for a common form of inherited colon cancer. He agreed to do a significant amount of media work, including press releases, interviews on morning network talk shows and a press conference. One result: hundreds of calls from families with histories of colon cancer. That was important not for patient revenue, but because the broader genetic pool of samples helped advance his research more swiftly.

6. Improving the Public's View of Science

Nobel Laureate J. Michael Bishop once told Sigma Xi, the Scientific Research Society, "While we struggle to balance the promise of science with social conflict, we must confront another challenge: disquiet about the stewardship of science. Fear, bewilderment, disdain; these are all opponents science must best. And there is one other, which is now current: mistrust."

People are wary of academics. They love your cooking but distrust your stoves. Better communications can begin to reverse those attitudes.

7. Communications Affects Reputation

Johns Hopkins, Harvard, Duke, Stanford and other educational institutions are expanding their public relations efforts to help in every endeavor from filling beds in hospitals to recruiting students and faculty. For instance, *U.S. News and World Report's* annual ranking of universities and hospitals is based mostly on reputation surveys. The magazine's ranking affects funding agencies, donors, recruiters and marketers.

You're the substance of what your university does. Being accessible, available, interested and prepared to be a credible source will build its reputation.

Positive name recognition creates a "halo" effect, helping build credibility not only for the individual expert source, but also for the institution.

8. Communication Affects Funding

As communication helps associate the name of your institution with excellence, it helps translate recognition into results and revenue. It helps recruit top faculty and students. It helps bring in money for government and private operating budgets and grants.

Congress and the National Institutes of Health, for example, are beginning to write requirements for public information outreach into the grant proposal process.

Convincing government officials to pay for research and education begins with public support, and it's clear people are demanding more accountability for spending than ever before. Building a base of support comes from getting your story out, not just through scientific and prestigious national publications, but also the hometown newspaper. The local paper is often the one that reaches the lawmakers who make decisions about whether you'll get the money you need.

9. They'll Do It Anyway

Journalists will pursue an important story whether or not you agree to participate. Helping is sensible self defense. The story is more likely to be complete and to represent your work accurately if you provide your expertise.

CHAPTER TWO

Why Journalists Act the Way They Do
Three Common Hypotheses and Four Standards

The process of news gathering and eventual presentation is to the writer what creative design of an experiment is to the scientist.

— National Association of Science Writers handbook

News is first of all a business, made up of commercial, profit-making enterprises. From small town weekly newspapers to major broadcast networks, bottom-line economics influences what kind of news is reported, how much is reported and how many people report it.

Before contacting journalists or responding to their inquiries, it helps to understand a bit of that business and how the news process works—how reporters report, what they consider news and the nature of their biases and limitations.

"News is both a product and a point of view," says George Hough in his text on news writing. A "product" because it's gathered, processed, packaged and sold. A "point of view" because it's also what a reporter, editor, reader or source considers interesting, exciting, important and timely.

As you would expect, there is no uniformity in the answers. Each journalist, publication and broadcast outlet has its own individual requirements and deadlines, its own perceptions about what's newsworthy. Fortunately there are a few consistent basics from which to start.

Kevin Hall, a former *Miami Herald* editor who now teaches writing at Florida International University, says a reporter's main task is to "find something of importance to people and share it with the greatest possible number at the earliest possible moment." This is probably as good a definition as there is for news and describes what journalists are after when they call.

Editors will tend to use a story, or give it more prominence, based on two criteria: importance and interest. The relative weight they give each depends on the news outlet and the audience they're trying to attract. For example, *The Los Angeles Times* gives more weight to importance; *People* magazine gives more weight to interest.

Because audiences tend to choose a program or publication based on how interesting they find it, more and more mainstream news organizations are choosing "interest" over "importance" in an attempt to raise circulation and ratings. Needless to say, the trend has ignited a great debate in and out of the business.

When editors evaluate a story on the interest-importance scale, they flash through a mental checklist with these kinds of questions:

- How new is it? A smaller but newer story will win out over a bigger, older story.
- How much impact? How many people affected by how much?
- How urgent is it?
- How unusual or unexpected is it?
- How close is it? (It's more likely to be news when it happens nearby instead of far away.)
- Is there conflict?
- Is there emotion? Does it evoke laughter, tears or outrage?
- How clear-cut or certain is it? (Editors prefer certainty and clarity.)
- Are there good pictures?
- Do competitors have the story? (A story's value rises when competitors don't have it.)

And then—sometimes—this crass marketing question:

- Does it tie in to one of our promotions, adjacent programs or marketing objectives?

But despite all the rules, in the end news is really personal and subjective. David Brinkley said, "News is what we say it is."

News is also increasingly specialized. There are nearly as many different types of publications and broadcast outlets as there are academics. There are more than 11,000 daily and weekly newspapers in the United States alone, but the number of specialized publications is even greater. It all adds up to huge possibilities for coverage of your work and your institution, and a chance for contact with a wide variety of journalists.

As you know, even general circulation dailies and weeklies are often specialized, segmented into "Living," "Style," "Business," "Food" and other sections, all with reporters covering those beats.

Daily Newspapers

In addition to daily newspapers published in most cities, there are "national" dailies, such as *USA Today, The New York Times, The Wall Street Journal* and a handful of others with circulation beyond the hometown.

Weekly Newspapers

Not all of the nation's 10,000 weekly newspapers are in small, rural towns. In fact, many white-collar bedroom communities surrounding the nation's biggest cities have great numbers of sophisticated, well-read weeklies covering local business, economics, technology, science and other news. Even a smaller weekly may assign someone to regularly cover the local university or other educational institution on a regular basis.

Wire Services and Syndication

In addition to the mainline *Associated Press, United Press International* and *Reuters,* a number of specialized news-gathering wire services have also emerged in the past few years, including ones specializing in business, scientific and international news.

Most papers also pay to subscribe to syndicated news services, usually run by large newspaper chains. For instance, a story published in *The Miami Herald* may be sent to other Knight-Ridder owned papers and Knight-Ridder syndication subscribers.

Magazines

The news stands are papered with specialized publications on virtually any subject from *Knives Illustrated* and *Hog Farm Management* to *21st Century Science & Technology* and *Wyoming Rural Electric News*.

Trades

Most professions have more than one publication serving their interests, often by sub-specialties. For example, there are more than 200 publications devoted to education, and within that broad category are hundreds of newsletters, journals, monthlies, weeklies and quarterlies distributed locally, regionally, nationally and internationally.

Broadcast and Cable

Opportunities on radio and TV are multiplying as the airwaves become increasingly segmented. In major cities, the radio dial carries multiple talk stations. Viewers choose from dozens of cable TV channels, including programming targeted to specialty audiences. TV news programming is increasing, from primetime news magazines to local all-news cable television operations.

It all means chances are greater that you may be called and asked to make a live or taped appearance on local or national radio or television. The initial call could be from a producer whose job is to line up guests, or from a reporter who wants to interview you in person or over the phone.

About Those Journalists

What will those journalists be like?

Some larger dailies and specialty publications employ reporters who are very well-versed in the areas they cover. Some science writers, for example, come to the job with Ph.D.s and an excellent understanding of a wide range of scientific subjects.

But most reporters are "word" people who studied humanities in college rather than math or science. Many are "general assignment" reporters, covering widely disparate subjects at a moment's notice.

What else can you expect? Here are three commonly held hypotheses about journalists:

Hypothesis #1
Journalists are trained to be skeptics, and often are not well-versed in the subjects they report.

Guilty. Journalists must be skeptical or else be taken in by anyone who talks a good story. And since they often deal with wide-ranging subject matter, journalists simply can't be intimately knowledgeable about everything they're asked to cover.

This is especially true in academic specialties where a journalist may be asked to write about the latest announcement in toxicology research in the morning, attend a press conference on astronomy at noon and do an interview with the university's poet-in-residence later that evening.

Smart journalists are aware of their limitations in covering complex issues, just as you're aware of your relative unfamiliarity with their business. Tolerance from both camps can go a long way toward helping build successful interaction with the news media.

Consider, too, the good side of a reporter's lack of "insider" knowledge. The reporter may be more objective, less afraid to ask simple questions, more likely to reject obfuscating jargon. When a reporter approaches a story with the naiveté of a consumer, consumers will be more likely to understand the final story.

Hypothesis #2
Reporters know what they're going to write before the interview.

It's probably impossible to be purely objective when gathering news, but most reporters try to remain neutral and fair. Journalists operate under broad, general principles of ethical conduct reflected in such documents as the code of ethics of the Society of Professional Journalists and under specific, written guidelines of most news organizations. Such codes of ethics hold truth to be the ultimate goal and set rules for gifts, conflict of interest and fair play.

As the foreword to the FACS book, *Journalism Ethics: Why Change?* reminds the profession, "Consciously or not, journalists practice ethics every day of their working lives. How much time to devote to a story, whether to include a name, whether to disclose a source, what to show on the screen: these are value judgments and involve ethical decisions."

Like all of us, though, reporters are not infallible. A "fairness" doctrine doesn't guarantee that you won't be misquoted or your research misrepresented.

Hypothesis #3
Journalists generally look for simple explanations, and often have little time or patience for detail and perspective.

Journalists reflect what they believe are the tastes of their audiences, and often that means cutting to the heart of a story at the expense of those details.

Audiences want to know immediately, "What does it mean to me?" They're often busy and distracted, anxious to grab what is important or interesting in a story and move on.

For the same reason, reporters often look for the "outrage factor," and concentrate on immediate, colorful or spectacular aspects of a story. They're likely to jump at a good quote in preference to duller analysis. They're trying to make a story interesting to the most readers.

Coping

Four standards can help you roll with the truth of these hypotheses, to understand and deal effectively with the news media.

Standard #1
Know the difference between "hard" and "soft" news.

Hard news generally involves what the public needs to know about emergencies, rapidly unfolding events or the results of crucial research. Some of the kinds of soft news are feature stories, background reports and personality profiles.

Hard news has short deadlines. Soft news has a longer shelf life and generally looser deadlines. In newsroom jargon, it's "evergreen"—it won't turn stale and brown waiting for publication. A story about continuing AIDS research is soft news. One about a breakthrough in controlling the AIDS virus is hard news and will get immediate, deadline treatment.

For you, the most important practical difference in the two is deadline urgency. Reporters on deadline are under intense pressure. You'll be more help to them (and be more likely to make it into the story) if you can meet their need for speed. On deadline, response is measured in minutes. Tomorrow or later this afternoon will simply be too late.

Standard #2
Know the differences in reporters and their understanding of your institution and your work.

Make certain you understand who's calling. Is it a "beat" reporter with some knowledge of your field, or a television or radio newsperson looking for a quick "sound bite," with little or no background in your subject area.

Be ready and willing to help, to "translate." Academics often have their own "precision of language," as Professor Kevin Hall likes to say. Some are reluctant or even loathe to translate for fear of ostracism by their academic peers. But if the story is incorrect, it's difficult to justify a complaint if you haven't done your best to help.

Standard #3
Know the requirements and demographics of the publication or broadcast outlet the journalist represents.

Becoming an effective news source requires more than being listed in an institution's press guide as an expert. It means being responsive and pro-active, tolerant as well as critical, and it means understanding the journalist's needs as well as yours and those of your organization. Knowing your audience is absolutely necessary when a news person calls on you, or when you initiate contact with a news person or organization.

It is useful to read or view the medium for clues to how subjects and sources are handled. For example, *60 Minutes* is aggressive, often chasing wrongdoing, looking for sources to dissemble or stonewall. *Science* magazine will be pressing for explanation and detail.

Remember, the jargon and code words familiar to your field which are appropriate for a professional trade journal will be a mystery to the audience of general circulation media.

Standard #4
Journalists cultivate sources who cut through jargon, turn a phrase, cite all sides, prove their research, respond quickly and are credible.

Once you've developed interview skills and established credibility with a journalist, you may find a sympathetic ear when it comes time for you to call about your research.

Surveys show that although many journalists give academic sources generally poor marks for accessibility and understanding of the news process, they also tend to trust those who have helped them with stories in the past. When you show that you understand how to cut through complexity and offer explanations that readers and viewers will understand, the journalist will likely be back for more.

CHAPTER THREE
Support Your PIO*
Nine Ways PIOs Can Help

Newspapermen often profess to despise PR people, yet I have found that those I can trust are often an immense help in the development of legitimate... news.

— Jenkin Lloyd Jones
Editor, *The Tulsa Tribune*

A few years ago, a molecular pharmacologist, Dr. Paul Talalay and his team at Johns Hopkins University, published a paper in the journal *Science* describing the discovery and isolation of a chemical found in broccoli that appears to have a protective effect against cancer. It didn't take a Nobel Prize scholar to know that the press and the public would love this story. What worried him was the potential for prematurely inflating the news. He had visions of people stripping supermarket counters clean of every cruciferous vegetable in sight.

* PIO (pronounced P-I-O) is short for public information officer, the most common, generic title for the person who does public relations work for the institution.

To help head off the hype, he worked with the public information office, approved an accurate press release and the plans for a press conference so that reporters could hear him say "caution."

To his delight, reporters for *The New York Times* and other major newspapers and magazines paid attention. Network television's interest was also high, fed by trays of broccoli and dip the public relations office provided as props. But it was a public relations call to the White House that guaranteed a good story and reduced the threat of a premature broccoli boom. President Bush's distaste for broccoli was famous. Might the new research persuade him to embrace the veggie? Bush's on-camera response, "I still won't eat it," was engineered by public relations people who knew the media very well indeed. And it helped keep the story in perspective; broccoli did not become the new oat bran craze.

Good university public relations and public information officers know how and when to create such happy "halo effects" to frame an academic story. They can also help you navigate some of the rough roads en route to good press relations even if you're an expert source of information.

They Know The Press's Agenda

Because they are in regular contact with journalists, read and watch the mass media, monitor coverage of competing institutions and read the media trade press, PIOs are more apt to know what's hot and what's not and which expert sources to match with which reporter.

In California, the *Orange County Register,* for example, has reporters who specialize in covering "malls," "car culture," and "social trends." Hundreds of journalists, including freelancers for magazines, specialize in science, the environment and higher education.

They Know The University's Agenda

PIOs try to keep track not only of *your* expertise, but also the issues and policies that need careful tending in the press. Among these are indirect costs, animal research, conflicts of interest, corporate relationships, marketing needs, AIDS in the workplace and minority rights.

They Can Gauge Timing In Media Relations

Working with the press is akin to traveling by airplane; if you don't know the schedule, you can easily miss the flight. The best PIOs recognize not only what makes news, but when it makes news.

Dr. Henry Wagner at Johns Hopkins, an expert on radiation working with yttrium isotopes, had tried and failed to interest the press in his work on nuclear energy development. Then came the Chernobyl disaster. His institution's public relations office quickly notified key reporters covering the Russian disaster of the expert's availability, and he was quoted widely.

Getting information out in a timely way is the key to a service-oriented media relations program that works over the long haul and builds reputations. Your public relations office can get news releases done in advance to help reporters prepare to cover your journal article when it is published. PIOs can arrange interview schedules to conserve time. They can organize press conferences to help assure the timely release of accurate information. They can make sure you don't call a news conference for 4 p.m. on Friday, since it would probably play to an empty house.

They Can Help Frame The Story

Over-stressed news people are more likely to respond to a well-packaged and well-presented story idea. Your PIO can help spot the newsworthy focus that will catch the imagination of a journalist. And with enough lead time, the PIO can help package the right story elements, attracting the reporter's attention by making the job easier. For instance:

- Can you find a "real person" affected by the story? Reporters try to include the human element and know that finding the right person can be time-consuming.
- Particularly for television, what visual elements can you put together to show what the story is about? How can you give it motion and color?

PIOs Should Know Where To Find Optimal News Opportunities

Without research that describes the media audience, it's difficult to know where your ideas will reach the people you most want to talk to. Public relations pros either have research information or know how to get it.

The research may very well show that small weekly and daily newspapers in your local community can serve your interests even better than an appearance on the network nightly news.

If you are trying to raise money for an endowed chair, it may be important to you and your institution that readers of *The New York Times Magazine* make a median income of $65,000 a year while *Investor's Business Daily* readers have a net worth of $1.1 million. If you're a political scientist with opinions about the effect of urban planning on local politics, you might want to know that C-SPAN may reach more of the nation's government staff than does ABC News. If you want to recruit women into a medical study, the *National Enquirer* is a first rate messenger for some socioeconomic groups.

PIOs Should Know Who's Who

If your PIO is really sharp you may find out that the health editor of *The Washington Post* is working on a special section or a breaking news story that dovetails with your work and interests.

The PIO may also be able to guide you on what to expect from reporters as you head into interviews. For instance, at *The Wall Street Journal,* more than half a dozen business writers cover specific niches, including technology transfer, entrepreneurs, patents or fraud, not to mention dozens of economics specialties. Whether one of these experts or a general assignment *WSJ* reporter is on your telephone can make all the difference in your response.

They May Know How To Leverage Your Message

The PIO should know if your institution has experts in fields related to yours, so that the university can get even better coverage and visibility for a given story.

For instance, a call from a religion writer asking for background about the Dead Sea Scrolls brought an entirely new story. The PIO arranged an interview with an archeologist in another department who worked on a dig in Jerusalem the previous summer. The PIO might also have suggested a feature story on a student who worked the dig, helping the admissions office compete for graduate students in archeology.

In another instance, C-SPAN called a university public relations office to ask for an expert to help with definitions involved in health care economics. The PIO probed the subject with the producer and the result was a live five-hour broadcast from the university. The program featured more than a dozen of the institution's leaders, including the dean and several tenured professors. Not only did it help the public understand the complexities of the economic aspects of health care reform, it provided a platform for the institution's many experts in the field.

Many public relations offices monitor on-line data base services, looking for inquiries from reporters who need experts to help them with stories. These offices are in touch with organizations that publish and maintain lists of expert sources promoted to thousands of reporters, such as ProfNet or the Media Resource Service operated by the Scientists' Institute for Public Information (SIPI).

Blur-a-torials Can Confuse

Today some news organizations blur traditional lines between news and advertising with so-called "advertorials," those special sections newspapers and magazines print that mix ads and ad-friendly stories. Sometimes these advertorials blur the distinction even further by omitting the customary "Advertising" warning label.

Advertorials exist because publishers find it easier to sell advertising in these advertising sections, and they make a lot of money from them. Most journalists think advertorials undermine the publication's credibility since the stories are usually written by the marketing department rather than journalists. They're typically unquestioning and uncritical "puff" pieces—stories that aren't representative of the organization's journalistic standards.

Even though the stories are uniformly positive, some universities and PIOs have taken a strong stand against participating in advertorials, believing the public sees through the practice and will think the institution less respectable for taking part.

For the same reason, they also stay away from the broadcast equivalent of the advertorial: the "infommercial." In this program-length commercial, TV stations tout university achievements for a fee, sometimes even using the station's news anchors to do the touting.

PIOs Collect Miscellany

PIOs often will know journalists who have a sense of humor and those who will take your witty quip and embarrass you with it. They'll know how to get a correction printed and even draft a letter to the editor or call the reporter for you. They'll know when and how to involve you in meeting an editorial board, going on a press tour or speaking to groups as varied as the American Society of Newspaper Editors or chambers of commerce.

PIOs field press calls, organize background materials, schedule interviews and notify others in the institution who are stakeholders in your efforts or related work. They'll work with you on presentation and interview skills and even take the gruesome animal jokes off the lab door before the camera crew arrives.

PIO Tips and Hints

Here are some tips to help you work better with your PIO:
- Let the public relations staff know when a paper you have submitted to a peer-reviewed journal has been accepted for publication or when you agree to make a presentation or give a speech. Provide the

PIO with galleys or drafts. Remember, nothing will go out without your approval, so don't be afraid to work in advance.

- If you can, find out the publication date of a journal article and let the public relations office know as soon as possible.
- Meet with the PIO to help prepare news releases, media memos or other background material for reporters. Offer visuals such as computer animation, photos, charts, models or drawings.
- Stay in town and be available to the press when the news goes out, and for a day or two after that.
- Respond to requests from reporters or public relations offices quickly, even if you can't accommodate them. They almost always work on a tight deadline. If you feel that you can't comment, let the public relations officer know in time to find another expert and to maintain a good relationship with the reporter.

Some Words Of Caution

The PIO is not there to "protect" you from the press or to give you "permission" to talk to reporters.

Many people make that mistaken assumption because of a common, reasonable (and misunderstood) institutional request that all press inquiries be "referred" to the public relations office.

The PIO is in place to help you make the most of opportunities, to help avoid mistakes and save time—to ease the process and help you prepare to meet the press. On a busy day, if the PIO is unable to respond quickly to a reporter on deadline, most will want you to set aside normal procedure and answer the reporter's questions.

CHAPTER FOUR

Specifics in Working With the Media
3 Dozen Ways (At Least)

In the absence of information, the media and the public will supply their own.

— Dani O'Reilly
University of Minnesota
Extension Service

Preparing for a videotaped interview, a scholar took just 30 minutes to explain four years of complicated research to a television journalist. "That was interesting," the reporter said as a camera crew set up equipment. "Now, can you boil that down to 20-30 seconds for me?"

This scenario is repeated every day, across the country, as broadcast journalists try to capture "sound bites" for their audiences. Even if radio and television stations had the luxury of conducting lengthy interviews with interesting people, they wouldn't have the air time to broadcast them. They want encapsulated, bare-bones snippets of information and opinion. Most have time constraints that force them to offer news in slim wedges stripped of complexities, designed to appeal to a broad-based audience.

Print limitations are severe as well. A lengthy interview with a newspaper or magazine journalist may often result in a line, a sentence or, at most, a paragraph within a larger story. Sometimes your quotes won't even make it into the story, the equivalent of being left on the movie-maker's cutting room floor.

Life is not without risk; your published words may be taken out of context, rendered incomplete, misunderstood, or—worst of all— accurately present something you wish you hadn't said.

Have you wasted your time doing the interview? Probably not. At the very least, you've gained experience in dealing with journalists and in expressing yourself succinctly about your work. You may also have established what could become a useful press contact.

In fairness to journalists, all but the tiniest minority honor accuracy and fairness. But deadline pressures and the limitations of time and space may lead them into inaccurate or incomplete reportage of your comments. As a news source, you can develop skills that will help improve the odds that you will be accurately represented in news stories.

One of the most important and mutually beneficial things you can do to prepare for working effectively with the news media is to take advantage of whatever spokesperson training your institution offers. No one expects all academics to have "star quality" and to be glib sophisticates in interviews, but the professionals in your public information office can help you to prepare for representing the institution, to do a good job of explaining your research and to be responsive when reporters call.

If your organization doesn't offer such training, either internally or through an outside supplier, at least have a colleague role-play the part of a reporter prior to an interview.

Author Clarence Jones believes that since faculty "are part of the media gamesmanship of the campus, (they) need to understand what the game is about." (Jones goes on to say media relations training can also help professors lecture more effectively, "deal with other faculty, speak to the Kiwanis Club and testify before a legislative committee.")

Kansas State University, for example, offers faculty and other university spokespeople a "Media Training Seminar." Florida International University calls its spokesperson training, "Hello, Professor, This Is *Nightline* Calling." And the media relations office at Florida State University offers a flyer called "The News Game...and How to Play It" to help faculty members cope with interviews.

If you've been fortunate enough to have received interview training, or have first-hand experience (good or bad), here are some suggestions culled from many sources that can help you further.

Prepare Yourself

You know your material better than any reporter does. That's obvious, but a point worth making. It gives you a leg up, but it shouldn't make you complacent. Have available simplified, brief, jargon-free materials about your work, both for a reporter's use and your own reference before and during the interview. Be prepared with handouts, video, graphs, pictures, whatever will help the interviewer. (Abe Lincoln is reported to have said that if he had only an hour to cut down a tree, he'd spend 55 minutes sharpening the ax.)

Determine Your Message

Anticipate questions and prepare for the unexpected. Know what you want to say and go into the interview with a few key points about the subject. Be ready for "the question from hell," or a reporter who is brand new to your area of expertise.

Know Your Interviewer

What publication or broadcast station does he or she represent; will it be "live" or taped; when and where will the interview take place; and what is the interview supposed to cover? You have rights here. Among them is whether you want to participate at all. You also have the privilege of getting back to the reporter when you've had an opportunity to think it over and gather additional information.

Practice Your Statement

This involves rehearsal. Get your notes in order, bounce ideas off colleagues, have a solid idea of what you're going to say in the interview and do one or more run-throughs.

Doing The Interview

Going into the interview, try to keep in mind what you'd like to have come out of it. If you could publish the finished article, or broadcast the television or radio interview, what would you and your institution want to see and hear? At the same time, however, keep in mind that you cannot control the result, only the kind and quality of information you provide. Reporters are after *news* and are focusing on what they believe their editors and audiences want.

Never Say "No Comment"

If you have to pass on a question, or if you and your organization would rather not talk about a subject right now, there are better ways to decline participation than saying "no comment." Remember Andrew Wiles, the reluctant mathematician. For example, you can simply explain your reasons for not doing the interview or answering a specific question. Or indicate that you'll get back to the reporter later, but only if you intend to. "No comment" gives a reporter the wrong signal and looks terrible in print.

Anything You Say May Be Used

Be aware that a casual question at the end of an interview can elicit an unguarded response you might not have given if you were still in the "formal" face-to-face interview. White House correspondents pride themselves in obtaining a small gem of a response as the President leaves a news conference. That quick response may well be something he later regrets. Let the unwary beware.

Unless you are thoroughly aware of the subtle differences among conditions like "off the record," "background," "deep background" and "not for attribution," it's best to leave the ground rules of the interview to your PIO or media relations professional. For more on these terms, see Chapter 7 and the answers to questions frequently asked by academics.

Help Guide The Interview

Speak to your audience, not the reporter. An interview is not merely a conversation. Keep your audience and key points in mind when speaking with a journalist. Other tips:

- Listen to the questions and think about your response; it's not just what you say but how you say it that often communicates your message.
- Don't use jargon. Simplify and personalize your responses.
- Make your key points first, even if it means taking your response beyond the question you were asked. With the time and space limitations, your key points may be lost otherwise.
- Don't let the interviewer put words in your mouth. Your answer will appear in print or on the air. The reporter's question probably won't.
- Don't hesitate to correct misstatements made by the interviewer. Do so diplomatically, but firmly.
- Tell the reporter you'll get back to him. The world isn't likely to end if you don't have every factoid at your fingertips.
- Always tell the truth. Lie to a reporter and your credibility and that of your institution is greatly jeopardized.
- Never argue with the reporter. Do not act combative. Maintain a positive attitude. Avoid defensive answers and hostile body language.
- Watch for misunderstandings. Offer added information. Ask if your points have been understood.
- Never ask to preview a reporter's story. Offer, instead, to review details or quotes. Occasionally, with complicated or technical stories, reporters are only too happy to have an academic interviewee go over material for accuracy.

- Determine what the reporter sees as the story. Do this at the end of the interview. What you hear back can tell you very quickly whether the reporter "got it," or missed your point(s). This dialogue with the reporter is seen as a "learning situation," and is almost always appreciated.

The Academic's Bill Of Media Rights

As an interviewee, you have certain inalienable rights when dealing with the news media. You can:

- Determine the time and location of the interview.
- Ask in advance about the direction of the interview and the subject matter.
- Set the pace of questioning and speed of response.
- Challenge questionable assumptions by the interviewer.
- Refuse to answer hypothetical questions, or to continue with the interview at all.
- Decide not to do the interview in the first place, after weighing the pros and cons (and perhaps counseling with your public information office).
- Respond to significant errors by calling the reporter, or writing a letter to the editor or news director, or asking for a clarification and correction.

Specific Tips for Broadcast

Practice. With or without media training, there are some things you can do to help ensure a successful broadcast interview. A little practice and feedback from colleagues, plus a review of radio or television taped interview, can help you prepare for the next time.

Radio

- Remember the "sound-bite." Be able to make your points succinctly, preferably in 15-20 seconds.
- Outline your key points (but don't read them).
- Ask the reporter if you are being recorded. You have the right to ask him to stop until you're ready.
- Speak in a normal, conversational tone, as though talking with a friend or explaining something to a student. But don't be conciliatory and risk sounding patronizing.
- Think about what was asked. Form a good response. Technicians can edit the space between the question and your answer. Even if it's live, they might run it again on tape later.
- Stand up when you talk. Even when speaking over the phone or into a radio mike, it's best to stand up. Your voice is heartier and you tend to be more alert and concentrated when standing.

Television

- Be yourself. Although television appearances make many people nervous, try to relax and remember to speak to your interviewer as naturally as possible.
- Talk to the interviewer or interviewers. Focus on the people asking the questions and speak to them as if

you're having a private conversation. In the TV studio, try to ignore all the distractions, including the cameras, lights, motion and people muttering over headsets.

- Sometimes these days you may not even be in the same room with the interviewer. On a live remote interview, for instance, the lens is the interviewer. You'll hear the questions in an earphone and be expected to talk to a camera. In these cases, view the lens as the eyes of the interviewer. Don't let your eyes dart around the room or stare away from the camera, since the effect on the TV screen will be unflattering.
- Be aware of your posture. Lean slightly forward in your chair, let your body language help communicate your message.
- If you have a chance, introduce yourself not only to the interviewer, but also to the production crew. If you're in a studio, it helps to meet the program's director.
- Dress naturally. Lean toward simplicity. The advance of technology has not changed the ancient guidelines against wearing lots of the color white or avoiding busy patterns. Solid blouses or shirts and dark-colored suits or blazers are best. Avoid bulky, jangly, sparkly jewelry (unless, of course, that's what you're talking about).

Follow-up Is Crucial

The interview is not over when it's over. "Debriefing" is a crucial part of good media relations—discussing with your public information officer how you thought the contact went. It means sending additional materials to the reporter if you agreed to do so, or if you thought of something he or she could use later. As part of your follow-up, check your notes to see whether you misstated something or need to clarify a point, then call the reporter to explain. Check the results of the interview in the paper or on the air and determine the accuracy of quotes and other details. Don't ask the reporter, however, to send you a copy of the paper or magazine, or a tape of your interview; arrange to get it yourself. If there are inaccuracies, consider whether a response is warranted. If the story is well done, consider writing a complimentary letter. It's an excellent way to build a positive relationship.

Make sure you keep a file of your media contacts. It might be a good idea to share these files with your public information officer.

Calling The Press

There will come a time you want to call a news organization, either on your own or through your institution's public information office. You'd like to publicize a grant or results of your research, respond to something in the local press or a trade publication or write something for a national news magazine or a newspaper op-ed page. Your initial contact should be with your public information office. (If you've established your own media contacts, simply consult with your PIO before you make your call or send your note.)

The test for initiating media contact is that you have news (remember: "timely," "interesting" and "local"). If you or the public information office have built credibility with journalists covering your "beat," there are several avenues for getting journalists interested in your views, your research and your organization.

Getting The Press To Call You

- Understand the news organization's needs, its deadlines and capabilities. Does it use photos, charts and graphs? Video, computer graphics or props? Do the reporters care about your subject? When do they need your materials?
- Offer to do an interview. Then use the skills you have developed.
- Get your expertise in print. Write a feature, an op-ed piece or a letter to the editor.
- Work with your PIO to create a news release about your work, award, conference paper or other noteworthy item.
- Prepare a "fact sheet." Develop other timely information items. Have a simplified outline of your work, or main points of your research, ready to fax or hand to a reporter. Some basic background information, arranged in "Who, What, When, Where, Why and How" style can be very effective in quickly communicating details of your subject.
- Notify the media. Tell them about a scheduled presentation, speech or other event that can be covered for print or broadcast, preferably the day it happens.

CHAPTER FIVE

Strategic Communications
Eleven Tactics for Big Issues

If you don't exist in the media, for all practical purposes you don't exist.

— Daniel Schorr
National Public Radio

Many academics want to have a consistent long-term effect on the public's perception of their work and to have the public's support.

The goal becomes what the American Heart Association's chief scientific officer, Dr. Rodman Stark, once dubbed "impact with *integrity*" (italics ours). With any label, it means disseminating information in an organized way over an extended period of time to enhance reputation and revenue. Clearly it's a much more effective approach than simply reacting to demands.

There are two steps:

- To identify overarching, important academic interests, issues, goals and policies.
- To distribute consistent and persistent messages about those issues to the appropriate (or "target") media.

Successful politicians have mastered this kind of strategic communication. The Clinton campaign's "It's the economy, stupid," became an instant classic of the genre. In addition to having skill selling burgers and mini-vans, some corporations are also adept at using communications strategy to influence public opinion on issues. The strategic communications program for Philip Morris, for example, doesn't defend the right to smoke per se, but the right to make choices about smoking.

At the Johns Hopkins Medical Institutions, the overall strategy for media relations is based on building appreciation, support and interest for discovery science. The tactics then support the strategy: Keep Hopkins medical and health research before the public each day, then combine that message with the idea that academic medical centers care about people and use tax resources wisely and creatively to advance knowledge on behalf of people's well being.

All Hopkins media activities are conducted with that strategic goal in mind, from defending lawsuits and protecting animal research to discussing conflict of interest policies, technology transfer, new buildings, executive salaries, or a new women's health service.

Strategic media relations can help raise money, recruit students and change behavior and ideas. "Social marketing" uses strategic communications to persuade people to exercise, eat less fat, preserve the wilderness, report child abuse, use seat belts and stay in school.

The Harvard School of Public Health wanted what all public schools of health want—to draw national attention to experts on preventive health and health policy.

Harvard faculty members created the Center for Health Communication and selected half a dozen target issues, with an eye toward what the public would find important, not just what the institution would find valuable. The list included seat belts, designated driver programs and anti-smoking messages. They then poured huge resources into positioning Harvard as an institution that not only cared about the public health, but reached out to do something about it.

Simply put, strategic media relations focus everyone's efforts in order to leverage, amplify and exploit press opportunities.

Academics can use the tools of strategic media relations to advocate and protect, to help shape public opinion and to disarm criticism of sensitive research areas.

Other uses:

- To build media trust and visibility as a credible and timely source of information on some subjects.
- To keep certain issues before the public. (The benefits of chemicals that may pose environmental risks, for example.)
- To help assure balanced, accurate coverage of issues important to you or your institution. (Support for space exploration or the National Endowment for the Humanities, for instance.)
- To expound on any cause that needs and justifies repeating. In recent years, those causes have included enhancing the professional reputations of musicians, psychologists and sociologists; explaining the commercialization of basic research and

scholarship; restoring faith in the nuclear energy enterprise; increasing financial rewards for humanities faculties; building public support for such academic interests as tenure, faculty retention, tuition increases, drug and dress policies.

Once you have a strategic direction, you'll need to develop approaches to support the strategy. Here are some ideas that you and your PIO can work on:

- Make a list of the issue or issues you care about and the individuals and groups you most want to influence.

- Tell your PIO about newsworthy stories that can carry the strategic information you want to communicate. Devise news "hooks" that will attract editors and reporters.

- With your PIO, develop mailing lists of general assignment and specialty beat reporters who care about your field. This can often be done simply by reading publications and noting the bylines of reporters who write about those issues.

- Develop a few news backgrounders, white papers or position statements that can help you and your media relations experts create editorial page columns, letters to the editor, or fact sheets for reporters.

- Send your name and list of interests to data bases of experts. Your PIO should know about these clearinghouse data bases.

- Be alert to news stories that can use your expertise. If there's an earthquake in Peru and you're a psychiatrist knowledgeable about the effect of mass disasters, make yourself available to journalists. (And if those reporters have turned to you in the past, they're more likely to ask for your opinion during a crisis.)

- Help plan press lunches, press tours or appearances on television or radio talk shows. It's easier to get time on local programs than on the networks, and they're a good way to polish your presentation. Use tapes of the local programs to "audition" for the national programs.

- Take advantage of local access cable programs. The audiences are often smaller than the average graduate seminar, but cable may be right for your needs.

- Offer to write a regular essay or column for your local newspaper or regional magazine. Social scientist John R. Lion appears regularly on the op-ed page of *The Sun* in Baltimore to write about mental illness, gun control and urban violence. Several physicians write "popular" press columns on subjects ranging from women's health to child psychology. A child psychologist who wanted to reach young children and their teachers with mental health information got *Weekly Reader* to run a weekly column.

- Get on the meeting agendas of organizations that are widely covered by the press or that can directly help you get your message out. These can include such professional groups as the American Society of Newspaper Editors or regional and local chapters of journalism associations like the Society of

Professional Journalists and the Radio-Television News Directors Association. Among academic organizations, consider the Association for Education in Journalism and Mass Communication or the American Association for the Advancement of Science.

The tools for strategic media relations are designed to work with other tools of strategic communication such as town hall meetings, door to door information distribution, brochures, public service announcements, advertisements and lectures.

Strategic press relations are a long game in a long season. Results may not be quickly apparent, but over time you will build your image as an expert source and an advocate who can make a difference.

CHAPTER SIX
Crisis Communications
Thirteen Ways of Making Lemonade

Blot out vain pomp; check impulse, quench appetite; keep reason under its own control.

— Marcus Aurelius (A.D. 121-180)

Unpredictable events drive much of the news, and sometimes you may be called on without much warning to react to breaking stories. You didn't ask for, plan for or approve of this. But suddenly, you, your institution, or your field of knowledge are in the spotlight.

Understandably, your first instinct may be to avoid responding until you can get your thoughts, your reason, your position and your approach under control. You may want to refuse to comment, arguing that to do so is "unseemly" or "premature."

In public relations specialist Robert Irvine's phrase, when news is breaking, "you are the headline," and the desire or determination to control or avoid the press can be fierce.

Experience shows, however, that there are compelling reasons for you to cooperate with the media, to discuss the agendas and interests of your discipline, your institution and the public that pays the bills. At times of crisis or high visibility—front-page breaking news—the public interest is even more compelling and the arguments for not communicating are less persuasive than usual.

Why?

First, when events are moving quickly, communication vacuums undermine authorities and experts, their disciplines and institutions. These are the times when, in Irvine's words, you suddenly "become essential to the future of your organization... Its perceived value will be determined primarily by whatever information you convey to board members, investors, customers, government officials, employees and other publics via the news media. Your statements will spill over and affect your entire industry."

Another reason is that when press and public demand for information is highest, those who are "missing in action" or "unavailable" become part of the story too—often perceived as suspect, cowardly, insensitive or obstructive as a result. Reporters rush into print with the "information" that so-and-so "refused to comment" or "would not respond to telephone calls or inquiries." They go around you to colleagues with less knowledge or an ax to grind, or quote politicians who want to cut your budget.

Chernobyl, cold fusion claims at the University of Utah, the explosion of the Challenger, Watergate, Bhopal, the David Baltimore research fraud case and the Exxon Valdez oil spill all became symbols of public betrayal. When certain people failed to share information—or the public perceived that they failed to share it—their action fed that sense of betrayal.

When experts refuse to communicate to the press at such times, they're usually afraid that anything they say will only make things worse, or they believe they can win the day by controlling access to information.

Sometimes that strategy works in the short run, but it rarely works for long. Consider the case of the hospital that for three days refused to acknowledge an outbreak of deadly meningitis in its newborn nursery, even after a hospital employee tipped off local news media. The hospital was afraid of losing patients, but in the end lost both revenue and community confidence. It faced critical editorials, demand for hospital investigations and lawsuits from families.

By contrast, consider a neighboring hospital that quickly called a press conference to announce the outbreak and the decision to close the nursery. It was rewarded with the confidence of patients, editorials of praise for its "good citizenship" and a reputation for credibility and "putting patients first." Did the second hospital lose some patients? Absolutely. But far fewer than the first and it didn't have to rebuild its reputation. Good crisis communication is good damage control.

These days, the same kind of process often comes into play when there's good news about a discovery or development in your field. In the age of instant communication, the press and the public have become accustomed to instant analysis of news. They want to know if the latest advance in some field is worthy of their attention, and they want to know how to assess the development, especially if it promises great benefit. If you're unwilling or unable to respond, your reputation may be affected just as it is in crisis.

So, what do you do?

The first step is to accept that control is probably impossible at such times. You can't predict, certify or guarantee what news agencies print or broadcast.

The second step is to use approaches that improve your odds of accuracy, balance and fairness.

An overarching principle to remember is that in times of real crisis, the public is looking for trustworthy information and—most important—emotional reassurance.

Guard Against Paranoia

News people are rarely are out to get you or your institution. Most of the time, the press just wants information that helps with a story. Just because a story or a reporter is not "friendly," or a journalist wants information you would prefer not to give at the time, doesn't make the inquiry evil or cynical.

At least initially accept press interest and urgency at face value. In the National Research Council's book *Improving Risk Communication,* the authors point out that "selling papers" and "sensationalism" rarely play a role in what reporters write. Indeed, "the reporter is much more likely to be motivated by events, by what other reporters are paying attention to, by information provided on a regular basis by sources he or she has cultivated, by deadlines and by what interests him or her as a citizen. The editor or producer will be concerned about the appeal and impact of the issue... as a whole...."

Provide Concise Information

Since the press is event-oriented, not issue-oriented, it won't work to lecture reporters about the grand, underlying issues when all hell is breaking loose.

When there's a Three Mile Island, Chernobyl or Tylenol crisis, reporters figure the public isn't looking for a tutorial on risk assessment or the probability of uncertainty, or why it will take so long to sort out the scientific "truth." They figure people want to know how it will affect them, how many are in danger, how much everything will cost and what the experts are going to do about it.

Guide Reporters

Reporters sometimes ask silly questions, especially when prodded by editors. Tempting as it might be to snicker and ridicule, it's clearly wiser to calmly explain the reasons you believe the request may lead nowhere. You may be able to reformat the issue or help the reporter understand why the question will lead to a dead end.

When news is breaking fast, reporters become even more impatient with arrogance and coyness.

Says Irvine, "Breaking news is no place for a foxhole mentality. The media are looking for someone who will be direct and honest. If you tell them what you don't know and what you do know, if you promise to get back to them with a statement, if you stick to your word and return their phone calls, the odds are that even if you can't give reporters exactly what they want, you will survive the onslaught intact."

Be Forthright

Say what you know. And if you've made a mistake, admit it and apologize. Imagine if Richard Nixon had admitted and regretted the Watergate break-in. Americans almost certainly would have forgiven him, and his presidency would have survived.

Tell The Truth
Tell The Truth
Tell The Truth

A well intentioned lie, a reassuring lie, a white lie or a lie by omission are still lies. During the famous Baby Fae case in which a child got a baboon's heart, medical experts deliberately fed the press misinformation to protect the family's privacy. It destroyed the experts' credibility instead. The press would have accepted an honest statement such as, "we want to protect privacy so we're not saying."

Announce Bad News

When you have bad news, announce it and keep some control of the moral high ground. Better to announce it your way, on your schedule, than to try to hide it or disguise it and have it come out later, laden with the weight of "cover-up."

Remember Your Real Audience

The press is a conduit to policy makers, opinion leaders and a variety of publics. When you offer your opinions, reassurances, expertise and information, think of the media audiences. Don't "posture" for your peers, your dean or your department chairman.

Show You Care

How well you communicate the value you put on people's feelings and need for information may determine your credibility for years to come.

When a young foreign-born physician contracted AIDS, a medical center was legally unable to assure him a job or a huge insurance settlement in part because of the physician's immigration status and state worker's compensation laws. Instead of explaining that to the press in regretful language and offering sympathy about his illness, the institution first stonewalled, then delivered its position in cold, legal language that guaranteed press sympathy for the physician and press anger at the institution. You can be "right" and still come out a villain.

Stick To Your Organization's Crisis Communications Plan

Most public affairs offices have crisis plans that establish where the press will be convened, served and even fed. They identify a spokesperson—or at most two or three—who will give consistent messages about institutional policy. They will identify the expert (you) and direct inquiries accordingly.

Prepare To Give a Crisis Plenty Of Time

If the breaking story is likely to go on for some time, plan to be available.

Be Fair To All

It's tempting to talk only to *The New York Times* or one dominant news agency or reporter when events are happening fast. It's tempting to think that the grateful reporter will be sympathetic and tell your side of things. It usually backfires. You won't get favored treatment and the organizations you ignored will be angry.

The reaction will be especially keen when experts ignore the local press in favor of the national or try to shut out "unfriendly" media in favor of pushover press. That's when the "outs" will go hunting for your hide and widen an investigation beyond your reach.

Stay Calm

When reporters cut off your thinking or ask you to repeat, or just aren't "getting it," it's hard not to be frustrated, especially when it's the 20th or 30th interview and you're exhausted. When the investigative reporter rolls in from out of town and asks biting, hostile questions just when you thought you'd explained all of that, think calm thoughts. Anger is trouble.

Winning in Crisis

A crisis is the most demanding, difficult time to communicate with the media, but also the most important. There is no better time to position yourself, your institution and your academic discipline as credible, trustworthy, important sources of information.

CHAPTER SEVEN

Nine Questions Frequently Asked by Academics

Twelve Reasonable Answers

> "Who are these people and why are they bothering me?"
> — Anonymous

If you've been keeping score, you know we're closing in on 100 reasons, hypotheses, standards and tactics for reaching the public through the news media. Still have questions? Here are answers to some we hear most often.

Q. Why are headlines often misleading?

A. Usually a problem arises because headlines are not written by the person who wrote and understands the story. Instead they're written by a copy editor who has to say too much in too few words. That's being helped by a trend toward more sub headlines (or "read-ins") that allow for more explanation of the story. Headline writing is an art, and headline accuracy is a perennial problem.

Q. **Why do some stories omit important information and not give full credit?**
A. There are three reasons: lack of space, lack of interest and the paper's style. Newspapers and magazines have more news than space, so they trim and tighten at the expense of completeness. Editors also know that most readers prefer shorter, simpler explanations and titles instead of longer, more complex—but more accurate— ones. They use their own stylebook "bible" or one from the Associated Press or *The New York Times,* and nearly all stylebooks make short shrift of certain titles and degrees. Even proper names are shortened. For instance, The Johns Hopkins University School of Hygiene and Public Health becomes simply Johns Hopkins.

Q. **Why must journalists have a story first?**
A. News consumers naturally go where they can get the news first—so newspapers or radio and TV stations that are first with a story gain audience. The best news organizations, of course, insist not only on getting it first but getting it right.

Q. **Who decides such matters as what to cover? What to put on page one? What to show on TV news? What to edit out of a story?**
A. News decisions can come from lots of people:

- For newspapers, and to a lesser extent TV, many stories come from reporters, particularly reporters covering an area of specialty.
- News and assignment editors determine which scheduled news events or breaking stories to cover.
- Managing editors and other top editorial leaders work with planning editors to decide which long-range reporting projects to develop or how to cover major special events.

In addition to using their own judgment about what's interesting and important, editors and news directors pay attention to audience surveys for clues to what the public finds newsworthy.

The process of deciding what to cover or how to use a story varies, depending on news organization. Typically, at least once a day, editors at most papers gather to determine the top stories that go on page one of each newspaper section and TV executives meet to choose the ones that begin television newscasts.

The reporter has the most say over what appears in the story, but copy editors on papers and producers in TV will often snip, change, suggest and cajole until the final product becomes more a collaboration than the work of any single person.

Editorial page editors determine the subject and content of editorials, which are written and researched by the editorial page staff. They rarely consult reporters, except to clarify facts. And, contrary to what many think, the publishers and station general mangers rarely get involved in daily news decisions.

Q. **How can I squelch bad information, correct errors and rectify wrong impressions?**

A. The best hope is to make sure a reporter has the truth before he types the story into the computer. Stopping things after that is virtually impossible unless you can make a serious case for national security, bodily harm or mistaken identity. Once a mistake is published or broadcast, you can use recourses ranging from demand for correction to letters to the editor to lawsuits. Work with your public information office to determine the best course of action in each case. Whatever happens, it's never as good as getting the story right in the first place.

Q. **What is a "sound bite" and how do I become one?**

A. The term came from the brief bites of comment sprinkled in television news stories, but now the jargon fits print as well. It's just a TV-style term for a quote, and the aim is the same as it's always been: make it so good it ends up in Bartlett's. There's no magic here, just practice. Look for metaphors, analogies, popular references and colorful language to make your complicated ideas accessible and quotable.

Q. **What does "off the record," "not for attribution," "on background," and "on deep background" really mean?**

A. Be careful if you're considering a foray into the murky waters of anonymity as a source. Know the reporter and be sure you go over the ground rules ahead of time. One of the basic rules: Make sure the reporter agrees to the terms *before* you provide the information. Don't try to put something "off the record" after you've said it.

Here are some basic definitions:

off the record means that what you, the source, tell the reporter will not be used in any way, shape or form. Many reporters, however, armed with what you've told them, will try to get someone else to go on the record with the same information.

not for attribution means that what you tell the reporter can be used but not attributed to you. If independently confirmed elsewhere, the information may be attributed to someone else.

background means that what you tell the reporter can be used in some context, but not for attribution.

deep background usually means that a reporter cannot tell even her mother that anything is known about the information you are providing.

Q. Why won't reporters let me check the copy for accuracy before printing?

A. Rarely is there time to get copy back to a source for checking in daily journalism. Many journalists, especially if they're reporting technical or scientific information, will read back to a source some material or quotes to check for accuracy. Some magazines and television networks also have "fact checkers" who will call back to verify information in a story.

A reporter's work is considered the intellectual property of that news agency. It is, therefore, inviolate and in need of protection from all outside changes or influence until published.

Journalists also know that human beings, given any chance to do so, will want to edit their own words, ideas and opinions. That urge is the result of second thoughts or a natural tendency to want to sound better or smarter. Generally, this results in a complete alteration of the content and course of an interview. Journalists are understandably reluctant to permit that kind of second guessing.

Q. **What is the Ingelfinger or Relman rule?**
A. This rule may be the most widely misunderstood academic source-journalist issue. The rule, named for either of the last two editors of *The New England Journal of Medicine,* says that a scientist whose work is on the press or accepted for publication by the *Journal* may not substantially publish the essence of his work in any other forum or publication. Other professional journals have adopted some form of this rule as well.

Critics, including many journalists, argue that the rule is used to intimidate scientists (especially young ones who need to be published to help their careers along) and keep their information out of the hands of journalists for unnecessarily long periods (sometimes years) until the journal releases it. Because of the Inglefinger rule, some scientists are intimidated into inappropriate withholding of information.

Example: Dr. Jones, following a public presentation of his latest study is asked by a reporter to explain a point. Dr. Jones declines, citing the Ingelfinger rule. If you, the source, have a paper "in press," you may not call a press conference or give your paper to *The New Republic*. But you can comment or explain. The rule does not apply in this example. It's foolishness to refuse to explain or clarify a point to a journalist in conditions which already have constituted publication before a room full of people.

Finally

Feel more confident that you know how this journalism craft works? Now it's time to set the book aside and to venture out with what you've learned. We need and welcome your wisdom and expertise in the public debate.

Bibliography

The letters M, J, P, S and U following some of the entries are an exception to standard bibliographic style and were inserted to assist academics in directing their further research.

M = media relations emphasis
J = journalism reference/text
P = public relations text/reference
S = science-writing book/reference
U = university/college/educational reference

Adams, William C. "The Role of Media Relations in Risk Communication," *Public Relations Quarterly,* Winter, 1992-93. M

Alberger, P.L., Carter, V.L. *Communicating University Research,* Council for Advancement & Support of Education, 1981. U

Baskin, Otis and Aronoff, Craig. *Public Relations* (3rd ed.), Wm. C. Brown, Dubuque, 1988; Chap. 10, "Media Relations." P/M

Biagi, Shirley. *Media/Impact: An Introduction to Mass Media,* Wadsworth, 1992. U

Blohowiak, Donald W. No Comment: *An Executive's Guide to the News Media,* Praeger, 1987. P/M

Burger, Chester. *"How to Meet the Press,"* Harvard Business Review, July-August, 1975. P/M

Burkett, David W. *Writing Science News for the Mass Media,* Gulf Publishing, Houston. 1965. S

Cater, Douglass. *The Fourth Branch of Government.* Houghton-Mifflin, 1959. U

Chambers, Wicke and Asher, Spring. *TV PR: How to Promote Yourself, Your Product/Your Service or Your Organization on TV,* Prima, 1987. P/M

Chancellor, John and Walter R. Mears, *The News Business,* Harper and Row, 1983. J

Cohn, Victor. *News and Numbers,* Iowa State University Press, 1989. J

Cutlip, Scott M., Center, Allen H., and Broom, Glen M. *Effective Public Relations* 6th ed., Prentice-Hall, New Jersey; Chap. 17, "Media Relations." P/M

Dunwoody, Sharon and Scott, Byron. "Scientists as Mass Media Sources." *Journalism Quarterly* 1959, Spring 1982. M/U

French, Christopher W. ed. *The Associated Press Stylebook and Libel Manual.* Addison-Wesley Publishing Co., Inc. 1989. J

Friedman, Sharon M., Dunwoody, Sharon and Rogers, Carol, eds. *Scientists and Journalists: Reporting Science as News,* Free Press, New York, 1986; see esp. chapters: "Physicians and Reporters," Dennis S. O'Leary; "What Makes a Good Science Story?" Joann E. Rodgers, Dennis O'Leary and Stephen H. Schneider; "The Scientist as Source and Author," Stephen H. Schneider; and "A Guide to Effective Communication With the Media," Neal E. Miller, Appendix A.

Gastel, Barbara. *Presenting Science to the Public,* ISI Press, Philadelphia 1983. Ch. 5 "Why Journalists Do Interviews, CH 6; "Preparing For The Interview." S

Goldsen, Rose. *The Show and Tell Machine: How Television Works and Works You Over.* Dial Press, 1987. J

Harriss, J., Leiter, K., Johnson, S. *The Complete Reporter,* Macmillan Publishing Co., New York, 1992 . CH 25, "Education, Research, Science," pp. 390 403. J

Hilton, Jack. *How to Meet the Press,* Dodd, Mead & Co., New York, 1987. P

Hough, George A. *News Writing* (4th ed.), Houghton Mifflin Co., Boston, 1988. J

Howard, Carole and Mathews, Wilma 1988 *Managing Media Relations,* Waveland Press, Prospect Heights, IL. "Not to Publicize Research," Louis West. M

Improving Risk Communication, National Research Council. National Academy Press, Washington, D.C. 1989. S

Irvine, Robert B. *When You Are the Headline,* Dow Jones Irwin, Homewood, Ill, 1987. M/P

Klepper, Michael M. *Getting Your Message Out,* Prentice-Hall, 1984. S/P

Kessler, Lauren and McDonald, Duncan. *The Search,* Wadsworth, 1992; CH. 8, "Experts and Where to Find Them," and CH. 9, "Interviewing" (tells journalists where and how to find experts, such as academicians). J

Killenberg, George. *Public Affairs Reporting* (Covering the News in the Information Age), St. Martin's Press, New York, 1992. (For views on how reporters are taught to think and cover beats, also see section, "Journalists and Their Sources.") J

Lee, Annette Hannon: "On the Record," *Currents,* March, 1992. (Council for Advance and Support of Education). U

Linsky, Martin. *Impact: How the Press Affects Federal Policymaking.* M.W. Norton, 1986. J

Martin, Dick. *Executive's Guide to Handling a Press Interview,* Pilot Books, 1990. P/M

McElwee, David A. editing coordinator: *Media Resource Guide* (5th ed.), Foundation for American Communications, Los Angeles, 1987. J

Miller, Neal E. *The Scientists' Responsibility for Public Information,* Monograph. Society for Neuroscience, 1979. S/M

Nelkin, Dorothy. *Selling Science: How the Press Covers Science and Technology.* W.H. Freeman, New York, 1987 S

Nelkin, Dorothy: *Science in the Streets, Report of the 20th Century Fund Task Force on the Communication of Scientific Risk,* Priority Press, New York, 1984. S/U

Rafe, Stephen C. *Mastering the News Media Interview,* Harper Business, 1991 P/M

Ramsey, Doug and Shaps, Dale, *Journalism Ethics: Why Change?,* FACS 1986. J

Rodgers, Joann, "Spread the Word, Why and How to Publicize Basic Science," articles in *CASE Currents*. Council for the Advancement and Support of Education. S/T

Reilly, Robert T. *Public Relations in Action* (1987), Prentice-Hall, Inc., New Jersey. Chap. 6, "Public Relations and Publicity," esp. pp. 162-64, "Some Media Rules To Live By." P/M

Rivers, William L. and Work, Alison K. *Writing for the Media*, Mayfield Publishing Co., 1988. J

Smith, Virginia C. and Alberger, Patricia L. *Communicating University Research*, Council for Advancement and Support of Education, Washington, DC, 1985. U

Sopow, Eli. Taking Charge! *A Survival Guide to Media Relations*, Media Scope, 1992. P/M

Strategic Communications for Nonprofits, The Benton Foundation and the Center for Strategic Communications, Communications Consortium Media Center, Washington, D.C. 1991. M/U

Weaver, David H. and Wilhoit, Cleveland. *The American Journalist: A Portrait of U.S. Newspeople and Their Work*, Indiana University Press. 1986. J

When the Media Call; A Guide to the Media Relations Office (pamphlets); Anderson Hall, Kansas State University, Manhattan, Kansas. U/P

Wilcox, Dennis L., Phillip H. and Agee, Warren K. *Public Relations* (3rd ed.), Harper Collins, 1992; "Media Relations," pp 266-67; "The Interview," pp 620-622. P/M

Wilcox, Dennis L. and Nolte, Lawrence. *Public Relations Writing and Media Techniques*, Harper & Row, 1990 (esp. "Working With the Media" and "Hewlett-Packard Media Guidelines.") P

About the Cover
Media Frenzy

Photographer Shmuel Thaler captured the look, feel and emotion of an encounter with the news media in this classic overhead view. New York Governor Mario Cuomo is at the center of the feeding frenzy, surrounded after his mesmerizing speech to the delegates at the 1984 Democratic National Convention in San Francisco.

About the Authors

Joann Ellison Rodgers became deputy director of public affairs and director of media relations for the Johns Hopkins Medical Institutions in 1984 after 18 years as an award-winning science journalist and columnist for the Hearst newspapers.

Rodgers is president of the Council for the Advancement of Science Writing and past president of the National Association of Science Writers, a lecturer in the Department of Epidemiology at Johns Hopkins School of Hygiene and Public Health and a frequent lecturer on science and the mass media.

Joann Ellison Rodgers

She is a Fellow of the American Association for the Advancement of Science, and served on the national Board of Directors of the American Heart Association and is on the national board of the Alan Guttmacher Institute. She is the author of five books.

William C. Adams is associate professor of journalism and mass communication at Florida International University in North Miami, Florida. Previously he was general manager, public affairs, ICI Americas in Wilmington, Delaware. At ICI (the American subsidiary of England's Imperial Chemical Industries) Adams headed the conglomerate's public affairs, including corporate advertising, media, government and community relations, sports marketing and corporate contributions.

William C. Adams

Prior to joining ICI, Adams served as public relations director for Phillips Petroleum Co. from 1978-88, and held media relations positions for AMOCO and Standard Oil of Indiana.

He a member of the College of Fellows, Public Relations Society of America. He belongs to the Arthur W. Page Society, the National Press Club and has held several offices in the Gulfstream Chapter of the PRSA.

Acknowledgements

Many people were involved in the development of the *Media Guide for Academics,* including FACS senior vice president Doug Ramsey and FACS publications director John Warner. Design is by Paul Rottler of DRS Associates. Two people were particularly helpful in providing input in editing: James K. Gentry, the dean of the Reynolds School of Journalism at the University of Nevada, Reno, who also serves as academic adviser to the FACS news source programs; and Ian Pearson, a communications consultant with 25 years experience as a broadcast reporter, producer and news manager, most recently in Houston and San Francisco.

Principal editor for the Media Guide for Academics was Mike Ferring, vice president of News Source Programs for the Foundation for American Communications. He has been a reporter, producer, owner, consultant and news director during more than 25 years as a journalist. He has headed the documentary unit of WCCO-TV in Minneapolis and the news departments of KOVR-TV in Sacramento and KRON-TV in San Francisco. Mr. Ferring and the news staffs he led have won most of TV journalism's top honors, including the RTNDA Edward R. Murrow, Peabody, four duPont-Columbia awards, and more than 100 regional Emmys.

Mike Ferring

About
FACS News Source Programs for Academics

Vice Provost David Goodstein of the California Institute of Technology questions a panel of journalists during a media education seminar, part of a continuing series the Foundation for American Communications (FACS) offers nationwide.

FACS News Source Programs for Academics are designed to give you a greater voice in the public dialogue—to help you bring your expertise to the debate. They can help you become more familiar with the workings of the news media, to better understand how to be a source for information and to more effectively communicate complex concepts to the general public.

FACS offers workshops and seminars on college campuses nationwide. Besides a discussion on how to work with the news media, the sessions include a dialogue among faculty, reporters and editors.

The **FACS News Source Programs for Academics** and the *Academic Media Guide* have been created with the assistance of a grant from the W.K. Kellogg Foundation.

Colleges and Universities interested in presenting a FACS workshop or seminar are encouraged to call for further information.

3800 Barham Blvd., Suite 409
Los Angeles, CA 90068
(213) 851-7372
Fax (213) 851-9186